AWESOME DOGS

Shih Tzus

by Kari Schuetz

BLASTOFF!
2
READERS

BELLWETHER MEDIA • MINNEAPOLIS, MN

Note to Librarians, Teachers, and Parents:

Blastoff! Readers are carefully developed by literacy experts and combine standards-based content with developmentally appropriate text.

Level 1 provides the most support through repetition of high-frequency words, light text, predictable sentence patterns, and strong visual support.

Level 2 offers early readers a bit more challenge through varied simple sentences, increased text load, and less repetition of high-frequency words.

Level 3 advances early-fluent readers toward fluency through increased text and concept load, less reliance on visuals, longer sentences, and more literary language.

Level 4 builds reading stamina by providing more text per page, increased use of punctuation, greater variation in sentence patterns, and increasingly challenging vocabulary.

Level 5 encourages children to move from "learning to read" to "reading to learn" by providing even more text, varied writing styles, and less familiar topics.

Whichever book is right for your reader, Blastoff! Readers are the perfect books to build confidence and encourage a love of reading that will last a lifetime!

This edition first published in 2017 by Bellwether Media, Inc.

No part of this publication may be reproduced in whole or in part without written permission of the publisher. For information regarding permission, write to Bellwether Media, Inc., Attention: Permissions Department, 5357 Penn Avenue South, Minneapolis, MN 55419.

Library of Congress Cataloging-in-Publication Data

Names: Schuetz, Kari, author.
Title: Shih Tzus / by Kari Schuetz.
Description: Minneapolis, MN : Bellwether Media, Inc., 2017. | Series: Blastoff! Readers. Awesome Dogs | Includes bibliographical references and index. | Audience: Ages 5 to 8. | Audience: Grades K to 3.
Identifiers: LCCN 2016034479 (print) | LCCN 2016043001 (ebook) | ISBN 9781626175600 (hardcover : alk. paper) | ISBN 9781681032818 (ebook)
Subjects: LCSH: Shih tzu–Juvenile literature.
Classification: LCC SF429.S64 S38 2017 (print) | LCC SF429.S64 (ebook) | DDC 636.76–dc23
LC record available at https://lccn.loc.gov/2016034479

Editor: Betsy Rathburn   Designer: Lois Stanfield

Printed in the United States of America, North Mankato, MN.

Table of Contents

Shih tzus are sweet little dogs. They are favorite **companions** to many dog lovers.

Their wide-eyed looks make their owners smile!

Small in size, shih tzus make good lapdogs.

The **American Kennel Club**
puts the **breed** in its **Toy Group**.

Shih tzus are known for their pretty hair.

Shih Tzu Coats

solid   bi-color   tri-color

Coats are often **solid** or **bi-color**. They can also be **tri-color**.

At dog shows, shih tzus
have long, flowing coats.

Their full tails sit high up. **Topknots** keep hair out of their eyes.

Underneath thick coats, shih tzus have strong little bodies.

Shih Tzu Profile

long, fluffy tail

large, wide eyes

short muzzle

Life Span: 12 to 14 years

Trainability:

1 2 3 4 5 6

Hardest to train   Easiest to train

Hanging ears and short **muzzles** also hide behind their hair.

History of Shih Tzus

Hundreds of years ago, shih tzus lived in palaces with Chinese **royalty**.

China

N
W
E
S

The dogs were valued for their lion-like faces. In fact, their name means "lion dog."

The dogs almost disappeared along with China's last **dynasty**.

But Europeans **bred** the
few shih tzus they had.
They saved the breed!

Princes and Princesses

In many ways, shih tzus act like princes and princesses.

They walk gracefully with their heads up. They seek out comfortable places to rest.

Families can count on shih tzus to be very **loyal**.

In return, the dogs need belly
rubs and a lot of attention!

Glossary

American Kennel Club—an organization that keeps track of dog breeds in the United States

bi-color—a color that has two fur colors, one being white

bred—purposely mated two dogs to make puppies with certain qualities

breed—a type of dog

coats—the hair or fur covering some animals

companions—friends who keep someone company

dynasty—a family of rulers in power for a long time

loyal—having constant support for someone

muzzles—the noses and mouths of some animals

royalty—kings, queens, emperors, empresses, and other rulers

solid—one color

topknots—knots of hair tied with bows or ribbons; a topknot sits at the top of the head.

Toy Group—a group of the smallest dog breeds; most dogs in the Toy Group were bred to be companions.

tri-color—a pattern that has three colors

To Learn More

AT THE LIBRARY

Landau, Elaine. *Shih Tzus Are the Best!* Minneapolis, Minn.: Lerner, 2011.

Markovics, Joyce. *Shih Tzu: Lion Dog.* New York, N.Y.: Bearport, 2011.

Morey, Allan. *Shih Tzus.* North Mankato, Minn.: Capstone Press, 2017.

ON THE WEB

Learning more about shih tzus is as easy as 1, 2, 3.

1. Go to www.factsurfer.com.

2. Enter "shih tzus" into the search box.

3. Click the "Surf" button and you will see a list of related web sites.

With factsurfer.com, finding more information is just a click away.

Index

The images in this book are reproduced through the courtesy of: Eric Isselee, front cover, pp. 5, 9 (left, center), 13, 16; Danita Delimont/ Alamy Stock Photo, pp. 4-5 (subject); Blend Images/ Alamy Stock Photo, p. 6; Daz Stock, p. 7; chaoss, pp. 8-9, 18-19; WilleeCole Photography, p. 9 (right); imageBROKER/ Alamy Stock Photo, pp. 10-11; STEPHEN CHERNIN/ EPA/ Newscom, p. 10; Andrew Rawcliffe/ Alamy Stock Photo, pp. 12-13; cynoclub, p. 14; Roman Zhuravlev, pp. 14-15 (subject); PlusONE, pp. 14-15 (background); Anna Goroshnikova, pp. 16-17; Marek Bidzinski, p. 19; Jenn Huls/ SuperStock, p. 20; Angela Hampton Picture Library/ Alamy Stock Photo, pp. 20-21.